DATE DUE

DEMCO 38-297

AFRICAN-AMERICAN
SCIENTISTS

African-American Scientists

by Patricia and
Fredrick McKissack

A PROUD HERITAGE
The Millbrook Press, Brookfield, Connecticut

To Dr. Charles Burnsides
with many thanks

Photographs courtesy of the Library of Congress: pp. 14, 19, 25, 29, 35 (both), 39; Schomburg Center for Research in Black Culture, New York Public Library: pp. 22, 41, 42, 45, 47, 56, 67, 74, 83; National Portrait Gallery, Art Resource, NY: p. 52; NASA: p. 58; The Bettmann Archive: p. 65; Marine Biological Laboratory, Woods Hole, Mass.: p. 71; AT&T Archives: p. 89.

Library of Congress Cataloging-in-Publication Data
McKissack, Pat, 1944–
African-American scientists / by Patricia and Fredrick McKissack.
p.   cm. — (A Proud heritage)
Includes bibliographical references and index.
Summary: Examines the lives and achievements of African-American scientists from colonial days to the present, including Benjamin Banneker and George Washington Carver.
ISBN 1-56294-372-3 (lib. bdg.)
1. Afro-American scientists—Biography—Juvenile literature.
[1. Scientists.   2. Afro-Americans—Biography.]   I. McKissack, Fredrick.   II. Title.   III. Series.
Q141.M36   1994
509.2′273—dc20   [B]   93-11226   CIP   AC

Published by The Millbrook Press
2 Old New Milford Road, Brookfield, Connecticut 06804

CONTENTS

ACKNOWLEDGMENTS

A book of this kind is always difficult to write, because of the volume of information that must be gathered, verified, organized, and then written. For raw data and date verification we relied heavily upon Vivian Ovelton Sammons's lists in *Blacks in Science and Medicine*. Also invaluable were the works of Portia L. James, curator of the Smithsonian exhibit "The Real McCoy: African-American Invention and Innovation 1619–1930," and Jesse Carney Smith, author of *Epic Lives: One Hundred Black Women Who Made a Difference*.

We would like to thank the Associated Publishers, Inc., of Washington, D.C., founded in 1920 by Carter G. Woodson, who made available articles written about African-American scientists and also provided an extensive bibliography on the subject, compiled by Janet Sims-Wood, Assistant Librarian, Moorland-Spingarn Research Center, Howard University, Washington, D.C.

We extend a special thanks to our friends at Chicago Public Library, Fisk University, St. Louis Public Library, University City Library, St. Louis Country Library, Washington University Library, Missouri Historical Society, St. Louis Board of Education. In addition, we are grateful to Dr. Lincoln Diuguid and Bebe Drew Price, the daughter of Dr. Charles Drew, for granting us interviews, and our sons John Patrick McKissack, who spent several weeks in Washington tracking down information for us, and Robert McKissack, for lending us his organizational skills.

Hats off to our editors at Millbrook, who gave us the opportunity to document the lives of these great African-American scientists. Finally, we must thank the inventor of the fax machine, for without it this book would still be a "work in progress."

Patricia and Fredrick McKissack
St. Louis, 1993

AFRICAN-AMERICAN
SCIENTISTS

INTRODUCTION

Equal rights were clearly defined in the Thirteenth, Fourteenth, and Fifteenth amendments to the Constitution, following the Civil War. But Southerners doggedly refused to accept blacks as citizens, and white supremacy organizations sprang up all over the South. By the turn of the century the United States was becoming a racially divided nation, supported by *Plessy* v. *Ferguson*, the Supreme Court decision that condoned "separate but equal" societies. But without justice, equality is only an illusion.

Separatism spread quickly during the first decade of the twentieth century, and to justify the action, black people were unfairly portrayed as a silly people, only capable of menial work. School texts and the popular media reinforced the stereotypes by excluding blacks. All but a few contributions made by African Americans were diminished, which further added to the notion that black people had done nothing worth learning about.

Young black college graduates were not allowed to compete with their white contemporaries for jobs on an equal basis. Math, science, and engineering graduates had it especially hard. But for a few rare exceptions, white companies denied black scientists and engineers employment regardless of their education or experience. Their employment options were limited to African-American institutions.

Remembering the rejection and disappointment experienced by their parents, teachers, and neighbors, young black students began avoiding advanced science and math degrees. Even though they were capable, the career opportunities weren't available. That, of course, created a dearth of black scientists. Then the lack of African-American participation in the sciences was used to perpetuate the inferiority myth. Unfortunately, that notion is a stereotype yet to be overcome.

There were a few black men and women who stubbornly refused to give up their dreams to be scientists. And, with or without help or encouragement, they dared to conduct research, solve problems, and through their work improve the lives of millions.

Overcoming several centuries of discrimination has not been easy. Much of what we know about the early scientists comes from the scholarly research of the great sociologist Dr. W.E.B. Du Bois and the historian Dr. Carter G. Woodson. They reconstructed African-American scientific successes that had been deliberately excluded from mainstream American history. If these scholars had not saved the stories, they would have been lost and American history would have remained an incomplete portrait.

African-American Scientists introduces some of these interesting men and women: mathematicians, chemists, physicians, and others. We have tried to place their scientific contributions within the larger context of American history. Some of the people in this book labored under the tyranny of slavery, oppressive segregation, and overt racism, while others faced more-subtle race or sex discrimination—or both. A few died in poverty, but a few amassed fortunes. No matter what their circumstances, all of the scientists presented in this book are important American heroes and have earned for themselves the reward of being remembered. And in so doing, they have challenged us all to reach for the stars.

Benjamin Banneker made his mark as
a self-taught mathematician and astronomer.

1

THE SABLE GENIUS:

BENJAMIN BANNEKER

There are many points from which to begin a narrative about African-American scientists. The voice of Benjamin Banneker (1731–1806) calls out from the pages of history, asking to speak first in defense of African-American intellect. "One universal Father hath given being to us all," he wrote Thomas Jefferson in 1791. "He not only made us all of one flesh, but that He had also without partiality afforded us all with these same faculties and that, however diversified in situation or color, we are all the same family and stand in the same relation to him."

Benjamin Banneker was the first African American to gain international recognition as a scientist. His story is unusual and exciting.

The framers of the United States Constitution failed to abolish slavery, so most blacks were condemned to a life of endless servitude. Even in the North, where some blacks enjoyed freedom, they were still restricted by racism and discrimination. In the last decade of the eighteenth century, New York and New Jersey were slave states.

Banneker, a Marylander, embarrassed most slaveholders, who charged that Africans were incapable of handling their own affairs. Banneker's success as a landowner and scientist proved that black people could be productive if they were free and unhindered by slavery.

Banneker's Early Life

Benjamin Banneker's ancestry interestingly begins in England with a girl named Molly Walsh. A wealthy farmer hired her to milk his cows. A testy cow kicked over a bucket of milk, but Molly was accused of having stolen it.

The girl was unable to prove her innocence, so she was found guilty and fined. When she couldn't pay the fine, the judge gave her the option of going to prison or going to America as an indentured servant. Molly chose America.

After working for the customary seven years, Molly earned her freedom in 1692. The twenty-two-year-old woman was industrious, so she soon earned enough money to buy a hundred-and-fifty-acre farm in Maryland. Then she purchased two African male slaves to help her farm it.

As they struggled against the elements, Molly and the two men learned to depend upon each other and became friends. Molly freed both men. One left the area. The other, named Bannaky—who was said to be the son of an African king—stayed on as a hired hand.

Bannaky helped Molly a lot, because he had brought many farming practices from Africa. Her crops grew strong, and the harvests were bountiful. While working side by side, Molly and Bannaky fell in love, and they were married. Since Bannaky had no last name, he and Molly formed their last name from his first: Banneker.

Even though they were frowned upon, interracial marriages were not uncommon during the colonial period. Although Maryland passed a law in 1664 forbidding marriages between blacks and whites, the Bannekers lived in such a remote part of the state that they either didn't know about the law or chose to ignore it. Seemingly, they had a happy and prosperous life together, farming and raising four children.

When Molly and Bannaky's oldest daughter, Mary, was about sixteen, she accepted a proposal of marriage from Robert, a native African who had been purchased off a boat in Baltimore. Some accounts suggest that Molly and Bannaky bought Robert and freed him so their daughter could marry a free man. Another account says that when Robert became a member of the Church of England and was baptized, his master freed him. All stories agree Robert was free when he married Mary Banneker. Since Robert didn't have a last name, he borrowed Banneker.

Robert and Mary Banneker settled at Bannaky Springs on a piece of land her parents gave them as a wedding present. It was there, in a small cabin, that Benjamin was born, on November 9, 1731. That was the year when Maryland blacksmiths began using wrought iron to strengthen and lighten farming equipment. Iron farm tools were widely used in West Africa, so scholars of colonial farming agree that slave blacksmiths probably taught their masters quite a bit about ironwork as well as farm implements. Better-designed tools such as iron plowshares and coulters (which helped plows cut the soil) helped small farmers like Robert increase the amount of land they could till.

Robert must have been as successful as Bannaky, because he bartered 1,700 pounds of tobacco for 120 acres from a man named Richard Gist. The new farm was located about ten miles from Baltimore, along the Patapsco River. That's where Ben grew up. It was a peaceful environment, and he stayed busy romping and playing with his three younger sisters. Having a loving family gave Ben a happy, secure childhood.

Unlike most other eighteenth-century African-American children, Benjamin Banneker was the son and grandson of free black men. His young mind was never troubled by the uncertainty of when he might be sold away from those he loved. No fear of punishment squelched his curiosity. No cruelty destroyed his chance to learn. Free to explore the world around him, Benjamin blossomed into a bright and inquisitive child, the darling of his grandmother Molly.

Right away Molly recognized that Ben had a way with numbers. She taught him to read and write, and when he was ready she enrolled him in a Quaker school. As he grew, Ben's interest in mathematics

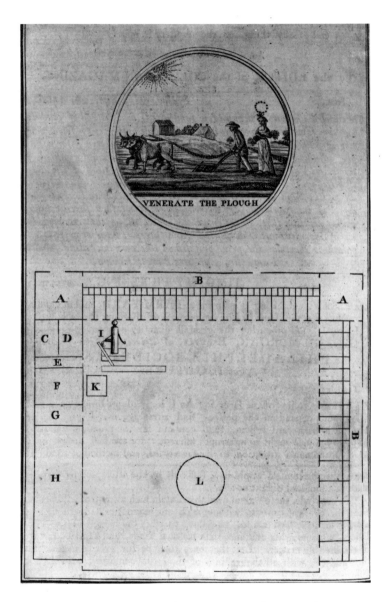

A plan of a colonial farm shows a farmer plowing his fields. Colonial farmers may have learned much about metalworking and farm tools from West African slaves.

expanded. When Robert or Mary couldn't find Ben, they knew where to look—out behind the barn or under a tree. That's where they'd find him scratching numbers in the dirt, or looking up at the night sky.

The Stargazer

Robert died in 1759, leaving his wife and Benjamin seventy-two acres. The remaining acres were divided among Ben's sisters, who were by that time married with families of their own.

The farm that Ben inherited from his father was described as "one of the best kept farms in the neighborhood . . . well stocked, containing select assortment of fruit trees, a fine lot of cattle and an especially successful apiary [a place where beehives are kept]." For Benjamin the farm was a means to an end. It earned the money he needed to continue his studies. He would rather study the nature of bees or the stars than harvest a crop. Some people thought he was lazy or perhaps a bit strange, but not George Ellicott.

While Robert and Mary were still building up their farm, Ellicott had come to Maryland from Pennsylvania. He'd built a flour mill and in time had become a very wealthy and influential man in the area. The Ellicotts were friends with three generations of Bannekers. Ellicott had watched Benjamin's growth, and now that Robert, Molly, and Bannaky were dead, he had become the young man's counselor and confidant.

Ellicott never discouraged Benjamin from learning. In fact, he opened his library to him, and the two men spent hours sharing ideas about science, math, and astronomy.

One of Benjamin's first projects was a wooden clock, which he built piece by piece. It kept accurate time for twenty years, and some historians believe it was the first clock of its type built in the United States.

When he was near middle age Banneker discovered the existence of astronomy, the science that deals with the study of all aspects of heavenly bodies such as stars, planets, comets, asteroids, and galaxies. A conversation about astronomy with Ellicott had challenged and excited Banneker. He knew nothing about the subject, so he taught himself about it. He read during the day and studied the sky at night. By then he'd lost interest in farming altogether, and he had rented the land to tenant farmers, leaving himself free to work on his new science project. He was particularly interested in the effects of heavenly bodies on the Earth's weather and tides and on events such as sunrise and sunset.

Quiet! Genius at Work

Within a few months Banneker had a working knowledge of astronomical theories and was able to detect errors in others' calculations. After a few more months of study, he was able to predict a solar eclipse in 1789. Then he decided to work on an almanac, which is a book containing a calendar of days and months with scientific facts about the phases of the moon, the tides, and weather. Almanacs predicted snowfall, rainfall, and other weather conditions and provided farmers with information about the best time to plant and the care of livestock. Compiling an almanac was no small

The title page of Banneker's almanac for 1794.

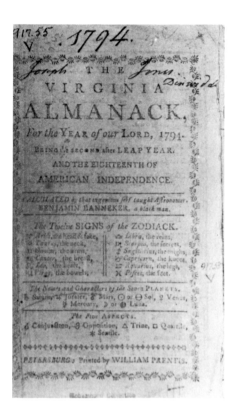

chore. It took patience and skill to make the accurate calculations needed.

Neighbors were surprised when they saw Banneker in a dark cloak lying on his back and looking up at the stars until dawn. He slept during the day, but sometimes he wrote. Few people, except perhaps Ellicott, understood that Banneker was not an addled stargazer but a genius at work.

He would work sometimes to the point of exhaustion, forgetting to eat and refusing to sleep until he had solved whatever problem he was working on. His sisters were worried about him and felt a wife was what their brother needed. But the confirmed bachelor graciously turned down several marriage proposals. In a letter to a friend, Banneker wrote that he didn't think it would be fair to marry a woman when she wasn't his first love (which was, of course, science and math). Banneker was single-minded when it came to his work. It consumed his life, so he chose to live alone, but he was not a lonely man. He was surrounded by plenty of nieces and nephews, with whom he shared many happy hours.

Planning the Nation's Capital

In early 1791, Banneker temporarily put his almanac on hold for a few months, because he was asked to do an important job for the United States government. President George Washington had set up a commission to design a capital city for the United States. A Frenchman, Pierre Charles L'Enfant, was selected to be the chief architect and head the capital project. Andrew Ellicott, the son of George Ellicott, and Benjamin were hired as surveyors and mathematicians in the planning of Washington, D.C. It was the first time an African American had received a presidential appointment for a scientific project.

Several government officials, including Thomas Jefferson, questioned the wisdom of including a black man on the team. Most of them, like Jefferson, were slaveholders. Abolitionists, however, used Banneker's appointment to support their position that slavery was wrong and needed to be abolished.

The Georgetown *Weekly Ledger*, dated March 12, 1791, noted the arrival of the team, which included, "Benjamin Banneker, an Ethiopian [a name used for African Americans at the time]." The article noted that Banneker's abilities as "surveyor and astronomer already prove that Mr. [Thomas] Jefferson's concluding that that race of men were void of mental endowment was without foundation."

Some thought that perhaps Banneker had been sent along to do a menial chore of no consequence. But even that notion was soon put to rest.

Midway through the project, chief architect L'Enfant resigned in a huff, returning to France with all the plans. The commission feared that months of hard, painstaking work had been lost. But Benjamin told Ellicott that he had memorized all the figures and calculations—and those he couldn't remember he could rework quickly.

When the commission members heard about Banneker's claim, they ordered him "to deliver to the Secretary of State, the Honorable Thomas Jefferson, a complete set of plans for the city of Washington and the District of Columbia." There were still those who doubted Banneker's ability, but his friends knew better. By using his incredible memory and mathematical talents, Benjamin Banneker reconstructed the plans for Washington, D.C., and laid to rest the idea that he was not qualified to be part of the survey team.

There were no wagging tongues on the day Banneker and Andrew Ellicott returned to Ellicott City in Maryland. They were received as victorious heroes, and George Ellicott was overjoyed. Banneker didn't seek the limelight; in fact, he was embarrassed by all the praise, modestly insisting that he had simply done his job.

Banneker slipped away from the celebration as soon as he could and returned to his house some miles away, where he was most comfortable among his books and papers, and the clock he'd made with his own hands. He was happiest when he was there pondering over a mathematical problem, writing, or sitting under an inky sky observing star paths.

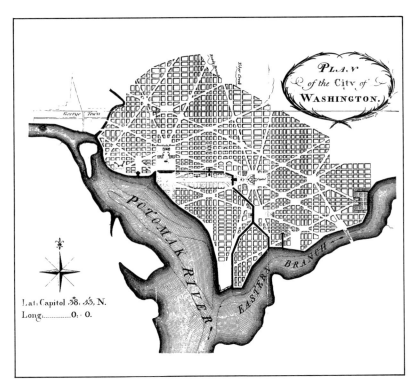

L'Enfant's plan for the city of Washington, D.C., was nearly scrapped when the French architect resigned in a huff. But Banneker was able to remember or rework all the necessary calculations.

He spent the rest of 1791 completing his almanac, but he couldn't find a company that was willing to publish it.

Thomas Jefferson had written earlier that, based on his observation as a slaveholder, blacks were "in reason . . . inferior, as I think one can scarcely be found capable of tracing and comprehending the investigations of Euclid [the famous mathematician of ancient Greece]." Jefferson's intellect was so well respected that his opinions were quoted as facts. So, if Jefferson said black people were inferior, whether it was true or not, it was accepted as truth. Banneker believed Jefferson's erroneous statement was at the root of his problem. He decided to challenge Jefferson by sending him a letter accompanied by a handwritten copy of his almanac, which, he believed, offered proof that a black man did clearly understand "the investigations of Euclid."

Banneker was familiar with Euclidian geometry, which is used in astronomy, and hoped that his almanac would convince Jefferson that his opinions about African Americans were incorrect. If a person of Jefferson's reputation publicly acknowledged a black man's work, Banneker reasoned, that acknowledgment would open doors for other black enterprises. Banneker wrote in part:

I suppose it is a truth too well attested to you, to need a proof here, that we are a race of Beings who have long laboured under the abuse and censure of the world, that we have long been looked upon with an eye of contempt, and that we have long been considered rather as brutish

*than human, and Scarcely capable of mental endow-
ments. . . .*

*Sir, suffer me to recall to your mind that time in
which the Arms and tyranny of the British Crown were
exerted with every powerful effort, in order to reduce
you to a State of Servitude. . . .*

*This, Sir, was a time in which you clearly saw into
the injustice of a State of Slavery, and in which you have
Just apprehensions of the horrors of its condition. It was
not, Sir, that your abhorrence thereof was so excited, that
you publicly held forth this true and invaluable doctrine,
which is worthy to be recorded and remembered in all
Succeeding ages. "We hold these truths to be Self evi-
dent, that all men are created equal, and are endowed by
their creator with certain inalienable rights, that amongst
these are life, liberty, and the pursuit of happiness."*

Jefferson's answer was more than Banneker had hoped
for:

*Sir, I thank you for your letter. . . . Nobody wishes more
than I do to see such proofs as you exhibit, that Nature
has given to our black brethren talents equal to those of
the other colors of men, and that the appearance of a
want of them is owing only to the degraded condition of
their existence, both in Africa and America. . . . I have
taken the liberty of sending your almanac to Monsieur
de Condorcet, Secretary of the Academy of Sciences, at
Paris, and members of the Philanthropic Society, because I considered it a document to which your whole
color had a right, for their justification against the doubts
which have been entertained of them.*

Banneker's almanac, titled *Benjamin Banneker's Pennsylvania, Delaware, Virginia, and Maryland Almanack and Ephemeris*, was published in 1792 by the Baltimore publishers Goddard and Angell. It included the usual information found in an almanac, but Banneker sprinkled amusing stories, puzzles, and riddles throughout it.

James McHenry, a member of John Adams's cabinet, wrote an article in which he praised Banneker's work as "fresh proof that the powers of the mind are not connected to the color of the skin."

For several years thereafter, Banneker published an almanac that was widely sought after and read. He and Jefferson continued their conversation through letters.

As he grew older, Banneker was honored by his neighbors. One friend described him as a man with "a thick suit of white hair, which gave him a very dignified and venerable appearance." He always welcomed visitors and fellow scholars, who came from far and wide to consult with him on scientific matters.

"Go to his house," another friend wrote, "either by day or night, there was constantly standing in the middle of the floor a large table covered with books and papers. As he was a mathematician, he was constantly in correspondence with other mathematicians in this country—including Thomas Jefferson—with whom there was an interchange of questions of difficult solution."

In addition to working on his almanac, Banneker studied and wrote about bees and locusts. Banneker stopped producing his almanac in 1802 at the age of seventy-one, but he lived to see the United States Con-

*The Capitol building in Washington, D.C.,
as it appeared about 1800.*

gress meet in Washington—the city he helped design—
and Jefferson become president of the United States.

One Sunday in October 1806, at the age of
seventy-five, Banneker went for his customary walk.
He died shortly after he returned. Honoring a request
Banneker had made, a sister gathered all his books and
papers and took them to Andrew Ellicott. Fortunately,
she acted quickly, because on the day of Banneker's

funeral, the log house that had been his lifetime home burned down. The rest of Banneker's possessions, including the clock he'd built, were destroyed.

Banneker had given another sister a feather mattress sometime before his death. Not long after he died, she noticed a hard spot in the mattress. Opening it up, she found a purse full of money her brother had placed there for safekeeping.

Benjamin Banneker presented a strong argument against the inhumanity of slavery, but whatever chances there might have been for voluntary emancipation were canceled when Eli Whitney patented the cotton gin in 1794. The invention made cotton the major southern crop and increased the demand for slave labor. Southern planters weren't about to allow anything to undermine their wealth and security—at least not without a fight.

IS THERE A DOCTOR IN THE HOUSE?
MEDICINE

The history of medicine does not begin in one place or with one culture. For many centuries, people treated sicknesses and injuries with a wide variety of curative potions. And for centuries, medicine and superstition went hand in hand. The familiar symbol of the medical profession, a staff with two snakes entwined, is based on the Greek and Roman myth about Aesculapius, a son of Apollo, the sun god. It was believed Apollo sent two magical snakes to his son with instructions to teach him about the healing arts.

In about the 4th century B.C., Hippocrates, known in the Western world as the Father of Medicine, began scientifically studying the human body and how organs function. He described many diseases and how they could be treated, but he is best remembered for the *Hippocratic Collection*, which contains what is called the "Hippocratic Oath," an ethical code of conduct by which a doctor promises to practice medicine. A modified form of the oath is taken by many medical school graduates today. In part the oath says:

The regimen I adopt shall be for the benefit of my patients according to my ability and judgment, and not for their hurt or for any wrong. I will give no deadly drug to any, though it be asked of me. . . . Whatsoever house I enter, there will I go for the benefit of the sick, refraining from all wrongdoing or corruption, and especially from any act of seduction, of male or female, of bond or free. Whatsoever things I see or hear concerning the life of men, in my attendance on the sick or even apart therefrom, which ought not to be noised abroad, I will keep silent thereon, counting such things to be as sacred secrets. . . .

Other cultures had advanced medical practices as well. Chinese physicians used acupuncture to relieve pain beginning about 2500 B.C. The Chinese knew about blood circulation long before William Harvey, the English physician, was credited with its discovery in 1628. And by the third century A.D., the Chinese had identified the cause of and treatment for vitamin-deficiency diseases, such as scurvy and rickets. The ancient Egyptians and the Incas of pre-Columbian Peru knew how to perform successful surgery on the skull, and physicians in the fifteenth-century West African kingdom of Song-hay were counseling women to space their children two or three years apart for better health of mother and child. And in the great cities of Timbuktu and Gao doctors were routinely performing cataract surgery.

It was in the Americas that centuries of medical knowledge from four continents merged. Native Americans, Asians, Africans, and Europeans each had their own ways of taking care of their sick and treating physical problems, and together those various methods formed the core of colonial medical practices.

Colonial Medicine

The African "witch doctor" and Native American "medicine man" have always been illustrated as wild persons dressed in outlandish costumes, wearing frightening masks, and equipped with bags of rattling charms and mysterious potions. There was assumed to be no science in their cures or remedies. Is it no wonder, then, that the witch doctor and medicine man were objects of ridicule and shame? Even the terms became synonymous with incompetence and chicanery.

But this is a distortion of the facts. Africans arrived in the colonies with knowledge of roots and herbs and how to use them to treat ailments. This knowledge was embellished by their contact with Native Americans and, later, Asians. It didn't take long for whites to learn that other cultures often had treatment techniques that were superior to their own.

For example, during the smallpox epidemic of

1721, Onesimus—a slave who belonged to one of Boston's prominent clergymen, Cotton Mather (1663–1728)—encouraged inoculation for smallpox. Onesimus described the successful use of inoculation in Africa. "People take the Juice of the *Small-pox*, and cut the skin, and put in a drop; then by 'nd by a little sick, then few small-pox; and no body dye of it; no body have small pox any more."

Cotton Mather wrote to his friend Dr. Zabdiel Boylston, asking him to support a widespread inoculation program. Boylston inoculated his son and two slaves with success, but people were frightened and allowed prejudices to cloud their judgment. Mather persisted, but his promotion of the practice drew harsh criticism. In Boston, Philadelphia, and New York, laws were passed to outlaw inoculations. A few years later, however, attitudes changed when George Washington had all his troops inoculated for smallpox, precisely the way Onesimus had prescribed it. But it was Boylston who got the credit. He was honored in London and made a fellow of the Royal Society.

Among the most respected members of the African-American slave community were preachers and "root doctors." The root doctor, though technically untrained, understood the curative powers of roots and herbs and used them to treat the sick. And far from being incompetent buffoons, root doctors were considered assets to both the black and white communities.

One slave master advertised for the return of a runaway slave named Simon in a 1740 *Pennsylvania Gazette*, stating that "[Simon] is able to bleed and draw

Boston clergyman Cotton Mather, who learned about inoculation against smallpox from the slave Onesimus.

AN
Historical ACCOUNT
OF THE
SMALL-POX
INOCULATED
IN
NEW ENGLAND,
Upon all Sorts of Persons, *Whites, Blacks,*
and of all Ages and Constitutions.

With some Account of the Nature of the
Infection in the NATURAL and INOCULATED
Way, and their different Effects on HUMAN
BODIES.

With some short DIRECTIONS to the UN-
EXPERIENCED in this Method of Practice.

Humbly dedicated to her Royal Highness the Princess of WALES,
By *Zabdiel Boylston,* F. R. S.

The Second Edition, Corrected

LONDON:
Printed for S. CHANDLER, at the Cross-Keys in the Poultry.
M. DCC. XXVI.

Re-Printed at BOSTON in N.E. for S. GERRISH in
Cornhil, and T. HANCOCK at the Bible and Three Crowns
in Annstreet. M. DCC. XXX.

Mather's friend Zabdiel Boylston, who wrote about the method, was generally given credit for developing it.

teeth" and "he is considered a great doctor among his people."

Slaves preferred to be treated by their own practitioners rather than white doctors. Eugene Genovese stated in *Roll, Jordan, Roll, The World the Slaves Made* that slave "hostilities toward white physicians had roots not only in an awareness of widespread ignorance and incompetence in the medical profession, but in their awareness that too many physicians used slaves as guinea pigs for their pet theories and remedies." But Genovese later noted: "Whites on the other hand were often treated by blacks throughout the colonial period and they [black doctors] were valued as slaves and as members of free communities as well."

Even after a law was passed in 1748 forbidding black doctors in Virginia to practice medicine on white patients, that didn't stop whites or blacks from using them.

In 1792 a black man named Cesat (or Cesar) gained such respect for his understanding of roots and herbs that the assembly of South Carolina purchased his freedom and gave him an annuity of one hundred pounds. *The Massachusetts Magazine, 1792*, noted some of Cesat's cures:

Sometimes an inward fever attends such as are poisoned, for which he ordered the following: Take one pint of wood ashes and three pints of water, stir, mix well together, let them stand all night and strain or decant the lye off in the morning, of which ten ounces may be taken six mornings following, warmed or cold according to the weather.

Cesat's cure for rattlesnake bite was:

Take of the roots of plantane or hoarhound (in summer roots and branches together), a sufficient quantity; bruise them in a mortar, and squeeze out the juice, of which give as soon as possible, one large spoonful; this generally will cure; but if he finds no relief in an hour you may give another spoonful which never hath failed.

If the roots are dried they must be moistened with a little water. To the wound may be applied a leaf of good tobacco, moistened with rum.

A Virginia planter wrote to a friend about relief he had gotten from the pain of rheumatism from a treatment his doctor had learned from slaves. And Fanny Kemple, a slaveholder, wrote in her diary about a female slave physician: "I was sorry not to ascertain what leaves she had applied to [my daughter's] ear. These simple remedies resorted to by savages and people as ignorant, are generally approved by experience, and sometimes condescendingly adopted by science."

Some of our most commonly used drugs are derived from African and African-American medicines. For example, the Bantu people of Southwest Africa used leaves from the willow and meadowsweet to treat headaches and stop pain and joint swelling. These plants contain acetylsalicylic acid, which was first synthesized by a Frenchman, Charles Gerhardt, at the University of Montpellier in 1853. Travelers had told him about its successful use by Africans. Forty years later, Felix Hoffman, an American chemist at Bayer, "rediscovered" acetylsalicylic acid—better known as aspirin.

The Right to Be Called "Doctor"

The distinction of being the first university-trained black physician goes to Dr. Louis (or Lucas) Santomee. He studied in Holland and practiced under the Dutch and English in New Amsterdam, which later became New York. Santomee received a land grant for his services to the colony in 1667. Little else is known about him.

DR. JAMES DERHAM □ Dr. James Derham (or Durham) (1762–18??) of New Orleans also distinguished himself in early American medicine. He was born a slave in 1762 in Philadelphia, where he learned to read and write. When just a young boy he was sold to Dr. John Kearsley, Jr., who employed him as an assistant in preparing medicines and attending patients. Kearsley sold James to an Englishman, Dr. George West, who was a surgeon in the Sixteenth British Regiment during the American Revolutionary War. Derham helped treat wounded soldiers on the battlefield, often risking his own life to save the lives of others.

After the Revolution, Derham was sold to Dr. Robert Dove of New Orleans. Amazed at how much Derham knew about medicine, Dove allowed him to work out his freedom by treating blacks in the area who had no physician of their own. By this time Derham was considered a doctor who had been trained by apprenticeship. This was all the training most physicians of that day had, because there were so few medical schools in the country.

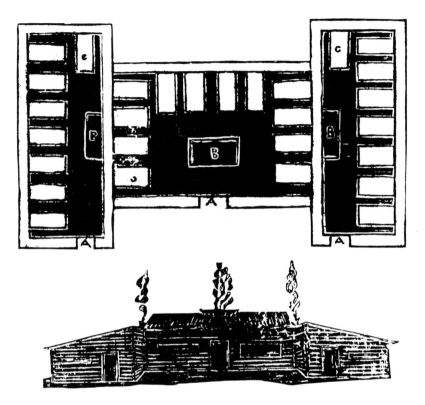

*During the Revolutionary War, James Derham
may have worked in a military hospital like
the one shown in this plan.*

Meanwhile, Derham's knowledge of medicine was growing considerably. His special interest was in how climate and diseases were related. Dr. Benjamin Rush, a well-respected white physician and friend of Benjamin Banneker, heard about Derham and was curious about him. Rush visited Derham expecting to give him some information about new medicines. "But he suggested many more to me," Rush wrote to a friend.

Rush read Derham's paper "An Account of the Putrid Sore Throat" to the College of Physicians of Philadelphia in 1789.

Derham, who could speak fluent French and Spanish, treated both blacks and whites throughout his career. A financial document from his records shows that he earned about three thousand dollars a year, a *very* high income in the eighteenth century.

DR. JAMES McCUNE SMITH □ Another early medical school graduate was James McCune Smith (1811–1865), who is best remembered for his writing and research. He attended the New York African Free School, established by the New York Manumission Society in 1787 to prepare black youths to become free and responsible citizens.

On his last visit to America, the Marquis de Lafayette, the French hero of the American Revolutionary War, visited Smith's school. Smith, who was eleven at the time, delivered the welcome address.

Smith's grades were so impressive that when he finished Free School, he went to the University of Glasgow in Scotland, where he graduated with a degree in medicine. He returned to the United States in 1837 and began his career in New York. His practice was large and included both blacks and whites, and soon he opened two apothecary shops (drugstores).

In the two decades before the Civil War, slavery was central to most public debate. Smith was brought into the discussion when he accepted the challenge to debate an opponent who believed that blacks were naturally inferior to whites.

*James McCune Smith
used reason and scholarship
to fight prejudice.*

At first, Smith thought the subject was ludicrous, for who could believe such nonsense? But abolitionists convinced him that the debate was important and his scientific voice was needed to refute the arguments of his opponent and all those who agreed with him.

Smith put his practice on hold and in preparation wrote "The Comparative Anatomy of the Races," in which he argued that when the skin was removed there were no anatomical differences between whites and blacks. Rather than becoming emotionally charged, he used scientific reasoning to counter all the arguments of slavery supporters. The debate lasted three days. In the end, Smith's scholarship won a victory for the abolitionist cause. But he didn't stop there. He helped disprove reports that insanity rates among blacks were higher than among whites, and that the African brain was smaller and weighed less than the white brain.

*Daniel Hale Williams, seen here as a medical
student in 1880, became the first American doctor
to perform open-heart surgery.*

Two of Smith's contemporaries were Dr. John De Grasse (1825–1868) and Dr. Thomas White (dates unknown). Both were graduates of Bowdoin College in Brunswick, Maine. De Grasse was the first of eight blacks to be commissioned a surgeon in the United States Army during the Civil War, and he served with the 35th U.S. Colored Troops in 1863.

The Medical School of the University of Pennsylvania, the first of its kind in this country, was established in 1765. But it wasn't until 1882 that Nathan Mossell became the first black man to graduate from there. Mossell founded the Frederick Douglass Hospital in Pennsylvania in 1895 and was the first black member of the prestigious Philadelphia Academy of Medicine and Allied Sciences.

Meanwhile, another outstanding student of medicine was studying at Chicago Medical College: Dr. Daniel Hale Williams, an 1883 graduate who, like Mossell, started a hospital.

DR. DANIEL HALE WILLIAMS □ Daniel Hale Williams (1856–1931) came a long way from his humble beginning in Hollidaysburg, Pennsylvania. After completing his work at Chicago Medical College, he served as a surgeon for the South Side Dispensary from 1883 to 1892. At the same time Williams served as a physician for the Protestant Orphan Asylum until 1893. In 1891 he founded Provident Hospital, the nation's first interracial care facility. It was also a teaching hospital that provided training for black medical professionals.

One night in 1893 a thirty-five-year-old man was rushed to the hospital with severe knife wounds in the chest. Moving quickly, Williams and his emergency staff treated the man, but the patient's condition worsened. If they couldn't stop the internal bleeding, the man would die.

Williams made a critical decision to operate. He surgically opened the patient's chest cavity—without the help of modern equipment or procedures such as blood transfusions. Although anesthetics and antiseptics were available at the time, they were nowhere near as advanced as they are today. Once inside, Williams discovered that the knife had punctured the wall of the patient's pericardium (the sac surrounding the heart). He repaired it, and the patient recovered and lived twenty more years.

Williams was the first doctor to successfully perform open-heart surgery in the United States. Williams was a pioneer in his profession, widely respected as a surgeon and for his administrative abilities. In 1893 President Grover Cleveland asked Williams to be the surgeon in chief of the Freedmen's Hospital, opened by the federal government after the Civil War to care for the newly freed slaves. For a long while the hospital, which was located in Washington, D.C., was the training ground for many well-known African-American physicians and dentists.

While at the Freedmen's Hospital, Williams set up various departments: medical, surgical, gynecological, obstetrical, dermatological, genito-urinary, and throat and chest. He returned to Provident Hospital in 1898 and served as a visiting professor at Meharry Medical College, in Nashville, Tennessee. At one time Meharry was one of the few independent medical schools run by African Americans with a full range of medical and

Provident Hospital in Chicago became famous for the pioneering work of Williams (upper left) and other African-American physicians, as well as for its nursing school.

dental programs. Between 1876 and 1976 nearly half the practicing African-American physicians and dentists were Meharry graduates.

Although he was given many honors and awards during his long career, Williams remained modest and, by all accounts, "a good and decent man, full of compassion." He was a founding member and officer of the

National Medical Association and a charter member of the American College of Surgeons, founded in 1913.

Williams inspired other African-American men and women to seek careers in medicine, and thousands more benefited from their contributions. For example, Dr. Ulysses Grant Dailey (1885–1961) began his career as a surgical associate of Daniel Hale Williams after graduating from Northwestern University Medical School in Evanston, Illinois. In 1926 Dailey started his own hospital and sanitarium, and for forty years he served as an editor of *The Journal of the National Medical Association*. Another young physician who was inspired by the work of Dr. Williams was Charles Drew, born in Washington, D.C., in 1904.

DR. CHARLES DREW □ Millions of people owe their lives to Dr. Charles Drew (1904–1950), who received a patent, on November 10, 1942, for an "apparatus for preserving blood which prevents the diffusion of potassium from the red blood cells into plasma." This medical breakthrough made the storage of blood in "blood banks" possible.

Drew was born in Washington, D.C., and excelled in academics and sports while working on his B.A. degree at Amherst College in Massachusetts. He was well liked by fellow members of the track and football teams and earned a letter in both sports. Drew also was awarded the Mossman trophy for his outstanding achievements in sports.

After Amherst, Drew attended McGill University Medical School in Montreal. Students and faculty at McGill were impressed with the scholar-athlete who, in addition to earning his medical degree in 1933, set

Charles Drew's research made it possible to store blood in "blood banks," saving countless lives. Here Drew leads other physicians on hospital rounds.

several track records and won a prize for his work in physiological anatomy.

When Drew graduated from McGill, the United States was in the grips of the Great Depression, and jobs and opportunities were limited, especially for black men. But Drew's credentials were so impressive he couldn't be denied. Drew found a job, but he went on to earn a Ph.D. in medical science from Columbia University in New York City in 1940. Between his studies, he followed in the footsteps of Dr. Williams by working at the Freedmen's Hospital. He was promoted to chief of surgeons and, at the same time, taught pathology at Howard University.

In the 1930s it was impossible to store blood for transfusions. Serious blood loss usually resulted in death. Early in his career, Drew began researching the properties of blood and its preservation. After years of work and study, Drew made the important breakthrough in blood preservation while working at Presbyterian Hospital in New York and at Columbia.

He discovered that by separating the liquid plasma from the nearly solid red blood cells and freezing the two separately, blood could be preserved. The patent application explained: "The core of the process resides in the centrifugal separation [spinning the blood rapidly so the heavier particles separate from the lighter] of the liquid red blood cells from the viscous plasma. When separated the two components can be frozen almost indefinitely and reconstituted in combination to form whole human blood."

At first, Drew's process wasn't received with a lot of enthusiasm by the American medical community. But the British military asked him to organize a blood bank in London during World War II, which he did between 1940 and 1941. With mobile blood banks set up close to the front, wounded soldiers could be transfused immediately, thus saving countless lives.

The success of blood banks in Europe paved the way for the formation of the American Red Cross Blood Bank, with Drew as the director. The American Red Cross was the supplier of blood plasma to American troops. For his work in this area, Drew was awarded the Spingarn Medal by the NAACP in 1944. This award is given annually to the person who has done the most during the year to advance the progress of African Americans.

After the war, Drew was given other awards for his work. All over the world, hospitals were using the process he had patented, but there was a lot of resistance in the United States. Some religious organizations rejected the idea of blood transfusions because of their beliefs. Many whites feared they would be "changed" if transfused with blood from a person of color. And there were just as many blacks who didn't want "white blood." The Irish didn't want Italian blood, Protestants didn't want Catholic blood, and men didn't want women's blood and vice versa, even if it meant saving their lives. Some people even mistakenly thought a transfusion from a wealthy or well-educated person would benefit them in some way. The ignorance about blood and blood transfusions was so widespread that private blood banks sprang up. It was common to see ads in newspapers stating "White Protestant blood only" or "Pure white blood available." All these prejudices overshadowed the fact that blood transfusions saved millions of lives.

To Bebe Drew Price, Drew was simply "Daddy." Price, the oldest of three Drew children, believes she inherited her father's sense of humor. Although he was extremely busy and was away from home often, Drew spent quality time with his family. "He was fun to be with," said Price. "I remember we built a doghouse together. When he was around we laughed a lot."

Price laughed, too, when asked how she got her name. Then she told this story. "My father was convinced that I was going to be a boy," she said, "so he never considered girl names." When told he had a baby girl, Drew asked the nurses to help him think of a name to suggest to his wife. "The nurses came up with Bebe," she explained, "Blood Bank! B.B. My parents liked it, and so I became Bebe Drew. That's my official name, not a nickname."

Drew returned to the Freedmen's Hospital after World War II and served as the chief of staff. He stayed there until his tragic death in 1950.

One winter evening Drew was driving along a North Carolina highway. His car spun out of control, and he was seriously injured. For a long while, the report was that Drew had been denied treatment and left to bleed to death at a rural white hospital. The doctors who were on staff at the time stated that they recognized Drew and, given their limited facilities, made him as comfortable as they could before he died. There are others who maintain that Drew was not given immediate medical attention that might have prolonged his life.

When asked about the circumstances of her father's death, Price answered that the autopsy records show that his injuries were so severe, there was nothing anybody could have done to save his life. "There is just not enough evidence to support the idea that a blood transfusion could have saved him," said Price.

A contemporary of Drew's was Theodore K. Lawless, a dermatologist.

DR. THEODORE K. LAWLESS □ On May 16, 1963, the mayor of Chicago and the governor of Illinois and a host of civic leaders attended a banquet honoring seventy-one-year-old Dr. Theodore K. Lawless (1892–1971). During the evening people spoke about the doctor's skill as a dermatologist and his outstanding work in the treatment of leprosy. But they also spoke about his philanthropic work. Lawless was not only a great scientist but a humanitarian whose reputation had earned him international respect.

Born into an upper-middle-class family in Thibodeaux, Louisiana, in 1892, Lawless attended some of the finest schools in the country, including Talladega University in Alabama, the University of Kansas, Columbia University, and Harvard. He received his medical degree from Northwestern University in Evanston, Illinois, and taught there from 1924 to 1941. Yet Lawless still found time to serve as the senior attending physician at Provident Hospital and to manage a private practice.

As early as 1929 Lawless had won the Harmon Award for outstanding achievement in medicine, especially dermatology. And he had earned a sterling reputation in Europe, where he made significant contributions in the treatment of syphilis, a sexually transmitted disease.

Today, Lawless would be called a "workaholic."

Theodore K. Lawless was as well known for his
humanitarian work as for his medical skill.

Even though he was a very wealthy man, he continued to work hard. Whether rich or poor, black or white, all his patients were treated with kindness and respect. When he wasn't treating patients or teaching, he worked at giving away large amounts of his money.

In 1956 Lawless donated a sizable sum of money for a dormitory at Dillard University, an African-American school in New Orleans, Louisiana. Dillard University also named the school chapel "Lawless Chapel," which made him smile whenever he said the name. He also contributed to the Lawless Dermatology Clinic, erected in his honor at the Beilinson Hospital Center in Israel.

At his testimonial dinner in 1963, the theme of the speeches was generally the same: Lawless was a generous person who loved doing for others, regardless of their race, creed, or nationality. What he gave to others, he received in triple measure all the days of his life.

Black Women in Medicine

During the colonial period, African-American women, as well as men, were respected root doctors. Sometimes called "conjure women" or "granny doctors," black women served as plantation midwives, delivering all the slave babies and, many times, assisting doctors in delivering white children as well.

The first African-American woman physician was Dr. Sarah Parker (Remond) (1826–188?). Sarah Parker was born in Salem, Massachusetts, at a time when women had very few rights and black women had fewer still. Women couldn't vote, hold public office, own property, or serve on juries. Elizabeth Blackwell (1821–1910) was the first college-trained white female doctor to practice in America. Like Blackwell, Sarah Parker had to leave the country to get her training, for no schools were open to any woman—black or white.

Parker studied at Bedford College for Ladies, in London, from 1859 to 1861 and Santa Nuova Hospital in Florence, Italy, from 1866 to 1868. She practiced mostly in Florence and Rome, Italy, returning to the United States to marry a Mr. Remond (his first name is believed to have been Charles) and to encourage other women to become doctors.

Dr. Rebecca Lee-Crumpler (dates unknown) and Dr. Rebecca J. Cole (1846–1922) were two of the earliest black women doctors to be educated in the United States.

Lee-Crumpler graduated from New England Female Medical College in Boston in 1864, a full fifteen years after Elizabeth Blackwell began her practice. Cole was a medical graduate of the Women's Medical College of Pennsylvania in 1867. Her practice spanned more than fifty years and included many honors and awards. The year Cole earned her medical degree, Dr. Ida Gray Nelson (1867–1953), the first black female graduate dentist, was born.

While these women made outstanding achievements, it is important to understand they were the exception and not the rule. Most black women were barred from the medical profession, except as midwives. It wasn't until 1879 that Mary Eliza Mahoney (1845–1926?), a midwife, became the first African-American graduate nurse.

Mahoney earned a nursing degree from the New England Hospital for Women and Children, started by Elizabeth Blackwell. Blackwell was a well-respected abolitionist and feminist who believed in equal opportunities in education for women and blacks.

Mahoney became interested in nursing when she was very young, and being the oldest child in a family of twenty-five, she had a lot of opportunity to practice her midwifery skills. She helped deliver several of her younger brothers and sisters. After graduating from New England Hospital, Mahoney remained in Boston, where she worked long and hard trying to promote good health care among women and children.

Although Mahoney graduated from a white nursing program, she was restricted from working in white hospitals. Pioneer black nurses were limited to employment in black institutions. By 1928, however, there were thirty-six black nursing schools. The oldest was at the Freedmen's Hospital. The Freedmen's Hospital Nurses' Training Program began on November 15, 1894. Two years later the first class of seventeen nurses graduated. Dr. Daniel Williams opened a school of nursing at Provident Hospital. Homer Phillips Hospital in St. Louis, Missouri, Hubbard Hospital in Nashville, Tennessee, Tuskegee Institute in Alabama, Hampton Institute in Virginia, and McLeod Hospital in Daytona, Florida, were also well-known black nursing schools.

Overcoming superstitions and ignorance was the most difficult task most black nurses faced. So to help organize black nurses and address health problems in the African-American community, Mable Keaton Stupers and others helped start the National Association

Adah B. Thoms was honored for her contribution to nursing.

of Colored Graduate Nurses. It combined with the American Nurses' Association in 1951. Every year the ANA gives the Mary Mahoney Award, honoring a nurse who in the spirit of Mahoney has made an outstanding contribution to nursing. Adah B. Thoms (1863–1943) was the first nurse to receive the award.

Contemporary women in medicine owe these women a debt of gratitude for the door they opened for them. One young physician who never forgets her history, yet has a clear vision of the future and her part in it, is Dr. Mae Carol Jemison (1956–   ).

In 1969, millions of people watched the historic moon landing, when Neil Armstrong took "one small step for man, a giant leap for mankind." Mae Carol

Jemison made a giant leap toward equality when she was one of two women aboard the shuttle *Endeavour*, on mission STS-47 Spacelab J, a cooperative effort between the United States and Japan, launched on September 12, 1992. She was the first African-American woman to serve as an astronaut and to be part of a space mission.

Jemison grew up and went to school in Chicago. Her father was a maintenance supervisor and her mother was a teacher of math and English. Mae graduated from high school at age sixteen and was accepted at Stanford University on scholarship, graduating from there in chemical engineering and African and African-American studies in 1977. After earning a Doctor of Medicine degree from Cornell University in 1981, Jemison joined the Peace Corps in 1983 and served in West Africa.

"I learned a lot from that experience," she told a reporter for *Ms.* magazine. "At twenty-six I was one of the youngest doctors over there and I had to learn to deal with how people reacted to my age while asserting myself as a physician."

Jemison doesn't have a problem asserting herself. She is very outspoken about women's role in space exploration. "More women should demand to be involved," she says. "It's our right. This is one area where we can get in on the ground floor and possibly help to direct where space exploration will go in the future."

According to NASA custom, each crew member is allowed to take along a few personal mementos on a mission. Jemison packed a poster of the Alvin Ailey American Dance Theater as a salute to creativity, several high school awards, and a few art objects from

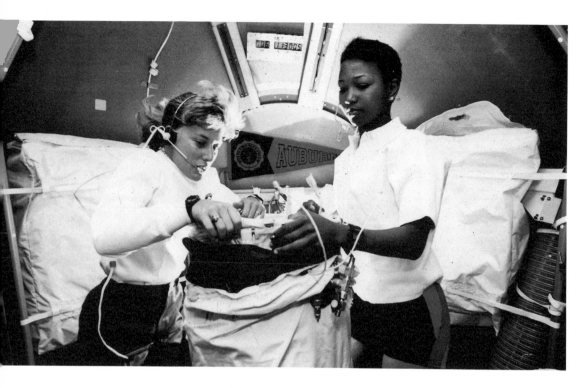

*Mae Jemison, physician, and fellow astronaut
N. Jan Davis prepare an experiment aboard
the space shuttle* Endeavour *in 1992.*

Africa. When asked to explain her selection, she answered with her usual candor. "I took the art along to represent those nations that are not in the space program yet." Jemison speaks passionately about her concerns for such nations.

"Space belongs to all the world, not just the rich, industrialized nations," she said. "We need more African Americans and Latinos in the field. We need biologists, who can put together parts of experiments; chemists for rocket fuel; and even lawyers who one day might write the contracts to determine who has mineral rights to mine the moon. If we're not there from the beginning, helping to determine what happens to these resources, we'll have no say in how they are to be used."

After Jemison leaves NASA, she plans to organize a program that will help prepare scientists in under-developed countries to participate in future space programs. In May 1993, Jemison took a step in a new direction when she had a small part acting in the futuristic television drama *Star Trek: The Next Generation*. Mae Jemison will always be remembered for her role in helping us all reach for the stars.

African-American Medical Firsts

Many African Americans broke new ground in medicine. Here are some of their accomplishments.

▢   David Ruggles, who was best known as an abolitionist, treated stroke patients with hydrotherapy (hot water under pressure) in the early 1800s. Today whirlpool baths are in standard use at most hospitals.

▢   Dr. Susan McKinney (Steward) (1847–1918) was the first African-American woman physician to practice medicine in New York and the third in the country. She was the cofounder of the Memorial Hospital for Women in 1881.

▢   Dr. Robert Tanner Freeman (1847–19??), whose parents were slaves, was the first black to receive a dental degree from Harvard, on March 6, 1867.

☐ Dr. Myra Adele Logan (1908–1977) was the first black woman to lead a team in open-heart surgery.

☐ Dr. Solomon Carter Fuller (1872–1953) was the first black to practice psychiatry.

☐ Dr. Eleanor Franklin (1929–) was the first woman—black or white—to head a university medical department (at Howard, 1963–66).

☐ Roseau Franklin Lee, who graduated from Howard in 1922, was the first African-American oral surgeon.

☐ Dr. John F. Burton (1913–) was the first black physician to be board certified in forensic pathology, in 1964.

☐ Herman J. Mabrie III (1948–) was the first black otolaryngologist—ear, nose, and throat specialist, in 1973.

☐ Dr. Augustus Nathaniel Lushington, who graduated from the University of Pennsylvania in 1897, was the first black veterinarian.

☐ Dr. Harold Freeman (1933–), an oncologist, helped start free breast-examination centers in Harlem that became models for low-income areas. The centers have saved countless lives.

☐ Dr. John Richard Hillery (1874–1940), a podiatrist from Maryland, invented the "Tarsal Arch Support" in 1929.

☐ Dr. Benjamin S. Carson was the youngest doctor to serve as the director of Pediatric Neurosurgery at Johns Hopkins University in Baltimore. In 1987, when he was still a resident, he assisted in the separation of seven-month-old Siamese twins connected at the head.

THE BIRDS AND
BEES AND
PEANUT BUTTER:

LIFE SCIENCES

In the area of life sciences—the study of living things—
there are two large categories: the plant kingdom and
the animal kingdom. African Americans have made
remarkable achievements in both categories, as bota-
nists, biologists, microbiologists, zoologists, bacteriolo-
gists, and specialists of many other kinds. One of the
most remarkable life scientists in the world was George
Washington Carver.

He never won a Nobel Prize, and he was never
accepted into the prestigious National Academy of Sciences, but when people speak about great scientists
George Washington Carver (1864?–1943) is bound to
be mentioned. His peers called him a genius, brilliant,

scholarly, "the Wizard of Tuskegee." But in his quiet, gentle way he always shook his head and said, "You must have me confused with some other fellow." His modesty only brought him more accolades. Known around the globe as "the peanut scientist," Carver left an indelible mark on American agriculture.

The Tuskegee Wizard: George Washington Carver

He began life as a slave in Diamond Head, Missouri, on or near July 12, 1864. (The exact date of his birth is unknown.) When he was just an infant, slave raiders captured him and his mother. Their owner, Moses Carver, followed them and found the baby left on the side of the road, but Carver never found the boy's mother. (Some accounts say that Carver caught up with the bandits and exchanged a horse for the boy. The slave raiders had already sold the mother.)

Since the Carvers had no children of their own, they kept George and his older brother. Susan Carver taught the boys how to read and write. As soon as he was old enough George's brother went out west. He was not heard from again.

George remained with the Carvers. He was a sickly child who stuttered when he got nervous. One day he heard there was a school in town. He wanted to go there, but "Uncle Moses" and "Aunt Susan" told him it was too far for him to walk every day. He was only eight and much too young to live on his own, but Susan Carver promised George he could go to school as soon as he could take care of himself.

When he was twelve and quite sure he was able to

take care of himself, George told the Carvers he was leaving. They were sad to see him go. After many years of hard work and struggle, George Carver graduated from high school and later college.

Although he was denied admission to Highland University in Kansas because he was black, Carver was accepted at Simpson College in Iowa, where he was the first black student to be admitted, and where, among other things, he studied art.

But George had loved plants and animals all his life. He was happiest when working with them. So he transferred to Iowa Agricultural College (now Iowa State University), changed his major, and received a bachelor's degree in agriculture in 1894 and a master's degree in 1896 (some sources say 1897). He was such an outstanding student, the university hired him to manage the college greenhouses.

While Carver was working his way through school in Iowa, Booker T. Washington was building a school in Tuskegee, Alabama. Like Carver, Washington had also been a slave, freed after the Civil War. He had received a teaching certificate from Hampton Institute in Virginia and taught there for several years.

In 1881 the general assembly of Alabama asked Booker T. Washington to serve as the first principal of a black school in Tuskegee. The first classes were held in a one-room shack with a leaky roof. When it rained, students had to hold an umbrella over Washington's head to keep him dry enough to conduct class. Many of his students were the children of sharecroppers who had little or no money for education. But if a student was willing to work, a way was made for him or her to attend Tuskegee.

From these humble beginnings, Tuskegee University grew. The young college stumbled along, with Washington steadfastly at the helm. Washington spent most of his time trying to raise money to keep the school going, but he also kept a sharp eye out for outstanding teachers whose educational philosophy was the same as his.

Washington heard about Carver's work at Iowa, so in 1896 he sent the thirty-two-year-old scientist a letter asking him to join Tuskegee's faculty as *the* science teacher and the director of agriculture. Carver agreed.

When he arrived at Tuskegee he wondered about his decision. How could he teach science? There was no science lab and no equipment. Although there was much to complain about, Carver decided to take action instead. He held classes in the fields, in the barns, and in the woods. "You learn by doing," he told his students as he helped them build their own lab from recycled materials they found on campus.

Once the lab was built, he turned his attention to the problems local farmers were experiencing. Based on the visible evidence of their poor crops, Carver decided to conduct a study. His findings were not a surprise. First, sharecropping was a system that worked in theory but not in practice. Actually, it replaced slavery in the South. Black farmers were kept miserably poor because unscrupulous landowners cheated them out of their "share" of any profits. But the Alabama soil was so overworked that the crops were poor. Most farms never made a profit anyway.

To make a bad situation worse, the boll weevil was ravaging cotton fields all over the South. The insect pest had brought southern agriculture to the brink of

Despite a rocky start—with no lab and no equipment—George Washington Carver created an outstanding science program at Tuskegee Institute.

disaster. The only way to bolster the sinking economy and break the endless cycle of poverty and failure, Carver decided, was to educate the local farmers. He held a series of farmers' conferences at Tuskegee, then went out on a horse-drawn wagon to the fields. From his "movable school" Carver lectured on sound farming practices such as crop rotation and land management. It was hard to get farmers to accept new ideas and change, but when they experienced success, they were willing to listen to more.

To help convince skeptics, Carver put his theories to work at Tuskegee Institute's experimental farm, which was operated by students. The farm was so successful that they produced five hundred pounds of cotton per acre, grew all the food for the college, and sold the surplus.

Once Carver had earned the farmers' and white landowners' confidence, he made a bold suggestion. Why not grow goobers (peanuts)? The farmers were surprised. The landowners were amused. Why? Goobers were fed to hogs. Africans had brought goobers to America and had grown them in small patches in the slave quarters. But nobody ever took goobers seriously as a crop. Where was the profit in growing peanuts?

Carver presented his case well. Peanut plants were immune to the boll weevil. Besides, growing peanuts would give the soil a rest and replace nutrients lost by overgrowing cotton.

But there wasn't a market for peanuts. Who would buy them, and how would they be used?

"Just grow them," Carver told the farmers, "and I'll find buyers."

Putting his reputation on the line, Carver set out to create a "peanut market." He worked in his lab night and day developing products made from peanuts, then invited several wealthy businessmen to have lunch at Tuskegee. When they had finished their delicious meal, he announced that everything they had eaten had been made from peanuts—the salad oil, even the ice cream. The hit of the luncheon was the peanut butter.

The businessmen went away convinced that investing in peanuts was a good idea. And that, of course,

Carver displays peanut milk and peanut cream, just two of the hundreds of peanut products he developed.

meant the farmers had buyers for their crops. There was much celebrating. Over the years, Carver graciously gave the credit to others, but everybody knew that George Washington Carver had helped save Southern agriculture.

For the next thirty years, Carver devoted his life to agricultural research, finding hundreds of peanut products—shoe polish, face and hand cream, shampoo, glue, floor polish, fingernail polish, ink, and many more. He also found hundreds of ways to use the sweet potato and pecans—including the making of synthetic rubber and material for paving highways.

Although Carver developed numerous products, he patented only a few of them, saying, "God is the Creator. I merely use what He has provided for us all." During World War I, German-produced aniline industrial dye was not available in the United States, so Carver used Alabama soil to synthesize organic dyes. These dyes were found to be superior to imported ones. He patented the process (patent #1,541,478) and a cosmetic he developed (#1,522,176).

Carver was awarded honorary doctorates from several universities, and was named a Fellow of the Royal Academy of England in 1916 for his contribution to agricultural research. He received a Spingarn Medal in 1923. His reputation spread so far and wide that Thomas Edison tried to hire him, but Carver chose to stay on at Tuskegee. Other large companies offered him money, position, and fame to work for them. But the gentle man who never married, never owned a house, and often forgot to pick up his paycheck turned it all down. Totally absorbed in his work, he had to be reminded to eat and sleep, yet he was always willing to talk with students and visitors.

In an interview, Estelle Pierson Smith, a 1937 Tuskegee graduate, recalled: "He was a happy person who encouraged his students to strive for excellence. I was one of his tasters. He would wave for me to come into his laboratory to taste ice cream or something else he'd made from peanuts. I had no way of knowing then how important Dr. Carver's work was or how fortunate I was to have him as a teacher."

Although Carver was a quiet man, he had a wonderful sense of humor and enjoyed a good laugh. Once, when he was to be given an award, the faculty bought him a suit because he didn't own one. When he was all dressed and ready to go to the dinner, he was overheard to say, "Do you think they'll recognize me without my white lab coat?"

Those who knew him best said he was perfectly content to work quietly in his laboratory, where Henry Ford paid to have the latest equipment installed. No one was surprised when Carver was given the Roosevelt Medal for distinguished service in science in 1939, or when he donated his life savings to set up the George Washington Carver Foundation. The purpose was "to continue his work for the benefit of mankind."

George Washington Carver died at the age of seventy-eight in 1943 and was buried in the campus cemetery. Thousands of people mourned him, including Franklin D. Roosevelt, who issued a statement saying, "[Carver] was a humble man who was a great botanist and agriculturist."

Many years later another president made a simple statement that sums up Carver's life and work. President Jimmy Carter, a Georgia peanut farmer, stated, "[Carver] was a genius."

Like a Fish in Water:
Ernest Everett Just

On February 12, 1915, the National Association for the Advancement of Colored People (NAACP) presented the first Spingarn Medal to thirty-one-year-old Ernest E. Just (1883–1941) for outstanding achievement in marine biology. Just wrote the NAACP a letter protesting his selection. He felt there were others who deserved the award more. But the selection committee stood by its decision, and Just was given the award. Just then graciously accepted it.

In the area of zoology and marine biology, Ernest Everett Just's name ranks among the highest. Between 1912 and 1939, Just wrote over fifty papers, published two books, and served as vice president of a zoological society. He was also the head of the Physiology Department at Howard University, in Washington, D.C.

Just was born in Charleston, South Carolina, in 1883, the same year the U.S. Supreme Court declared the Civil Rights Act of 1875 unconstitutional and fifty-three blacks were reported lynched in the United States.

Just attended public schools, then entered the state school for blacks at Orangeburg. Not long afterward, he transferred to Kimball Union Academy at Meriden, New Hampshire. Although he had very little encouragement, he was determined to finish. He finally earned his B.A. degree in biology (with honors) from Dartmouth College in 1907.

Then he was asked to join the faculty at Howard University. The school had been founded in 1867 to help educate former slaves. Today the university proudly boasts that almost half of the nation's black physicians, surgeons, dentists, engineers, and architects are Howard graduates. Just became part of the university's long history of excellence in its faculty. While at Howard, he became known as a brilliant researcher and a pioneer in the field of egg fertilization and the study of the cell. It was for his work at Howard that he received the Spingarn Award. Usually this award is

Ernest Everett Just at the Marine Biological Laboratory in Woods Hole, Massachusetts, where he did some of his important early work.

given to people at the height or even the end of a long career. In 1915, when he won the award, Just's career was only beginning.

While teaching at Howard, Just continued his education. By attending classes in the summer at the University of Chicago, he earned his doctorate in zoology in 1916. He returned to Howard, where during the school year he taught and continued his research in fertilization and cell division. He spent his summers at Woods Hole, Massachusetts, which at that time was a lodge where some of the most respected scientists came to study aquatic life.

While working at the Marine Biological Laboratory at Woods Hole, Just became interested in marine biology and narrowed the focus of his research to the artificial fertilization of fish eggs and experimental parthenogenesis, the development of fish eggs without fertilization. His books, *Basic Methods for Experiments in Eggs and Marine Animals* and *The Biology of the Cell Surface*, were required reading for biology students all over the world.

Through his scholarship he became one of the board members of the laboratory. He was elected vice president of the American Society of Zoologists in 1930, and in 1936 he was accepted as a member of the Washington Academy of Sciences. But he was still hampered by racial discrimination and prejudice. Like many African Americans at that time, Just found it easier to work and live in Europe where racism was not nearly the problem that it was in the United States.

In 1933, he accepted a grant to study in Berlin, and later, Paris and Naples. He lived in Europe until 1939, then returned to the United States and worked the remainder of his life as an editor of several scientific publications.

Dr. Charles Drew stated that Just was "a biologist of unusual skill and the greatest of our original thinkers in the field." Just was only in his late fifties when he died in 1941, but he is honored as one of the best in his area of study.

B Is for Bee: Charles Henry Turner

Charles Henry Turner (1867–1923) earned his Ph.D. in biology from the University of Chicago in 1907, the same year Just earned his undergraduate degree. In fact they knew each other and were good friends. While Just focused his work on aquatic life, Turner was most comfortable studying the behavior of bees, ants, and wasps.

Mae Turner Spencer, Turner's oldest daughter, remembered her father in a 1979 interview with the St. Louis *Globe-Democrat*. "We [children] had to live with voluminous books and laboratory specimens of ants, bees, roaches, snakes and other creatures. But, to me, my father was just a plain, kind man who instilled in us those qualities that would make for the simple, successful life."

Carter G. Woodson stated, "The late Dr. Charles H. Turner of St. Louis made an all but universal reputation for himself in the studies of animal behavior."

Turner was born into a black middle-class family in Cincinnati, Ohio, two years after the Civil War ended. He was an inquisitive child, full of questions about his world. "Do honey bees see colors? . . . Can ants hear

Charles Henry Turner was an authority on the behavior of ants and bees.

our footsteps? . . . Do bees have a language?'' Thomas and Addie Turner lovingly encouraged their son to find his own answers. So Turner worked his way through the University of Cincinnati looking for answers. After receiving a bachelor's degree in 1891 and a master of science degree the following year, he taught in the biology department there. But Turner saw a lot of things that disturbed him.

In the 1890s there were almost nine million blacks living in a U.S. society that was growing more hostile toward them every year. Black voting rights were under attack. Educational institutions were becoming segregated, and job opportunities for young black graduates were limited. Black leaders were concerned about the future. So in April 1893, Turner wrote a letter to Booker T. Washington at Tuskegee Institute in Alabama. "I am a colored man," he wrote, "and at present am teaching at the University of Cincinnati (white). I am anxious to work among my own people . . . and was informed you might know of an opening."

It is not known whether Washington helped or not, but from 1893 to 1905, Turner taught biology and chaired the science department at Clark College in Atlanta, Georgia. He was in the audience the day Booker T. Washington delivered the famous "Atlanta Compromise" speech at the Cotton States Exposition in Atlanta.

Booker T. Washington was well known for his industrial school philosophy, so he was invited to speak at the opening program of the exposition. His speech surprised many people. At a time when blacks were losing their rights, Washington seemed to advocate segregation in his speech. In part he said, "The wisest among my race understand that the agitation of questions of social equality is the extremest folly, and that progress in the enjoyment of all the privileges that will come to us must be the result of severe and constant struggle rather than of artificial forcing." He held up his hand and said that the races could be as separate as the fingers of the hand in all things social. Then he made a fist, adding that the races could be as one in times of national need.

Overnight, Washington became a national leader. Whites believed his was a course that all blacks should follow, but not all blacks agreed. Among those who did not was W.E.B. Du Bois, a graduate of Harvard University, who was teaching sociology at Atlanta University while Turner was at Clark. Du Bois wrote his opposing views in *The Souls of Black Folk*, in 1903.

The African-American intellectual community was divided into two camps: those who sided with

Washington and those who rallied around Du Bois, who was a founder of the National Association for the Advancement of Colored People and the first editor of *The Crisis*, the literary arm of the organization.

Where Turner stood with regard to these two opposing philosophies is not known. But records show that he was a member of the NAACP.

Between working as a teacher and principal at black schools in Georgia and Tennessee, Turner earned his Ph.D. at the University of Chicago and graduated summa cum laude (with highest honors).

He wanted to conduct research, but he had no money and a family to support, so he applied for a high school teaching position in St. Louis. He was hired to teach science at Sumner High School for $1,080 per year. When asked why he had passed up a professorship offered to him at the University of Chicago, Dr. Turner replied, "I feel that I am needed here [at Sumner High] and I can do so much more for my people."

On May 27–30 and July 1–3, 1917, there were race riots in East St. Louis, on the Illinois side of the Mississippi River. Turner was shocked and appalled at the senseless violence. Whites went through the community burning black homes and businesses, shooting, beating, and killing men, women, and children. Newspapers were filled with horror stories about the wounded and dead. Eyewitnesses saw the bodies of dead black people thrown into a morgue "like so many dead hogs." All told, there were "three hundred and twelve buildings and forty-four railroad freight cars and their contents destroyed by fire."

Turner wondered what caused ordinary people to become like crazed animals, stalking and killing without compassion. Once again he looked for answers among his insects. He observed them in their natural environment and in control colonies set up in his home laboratory. By observing their movements, Turner chronicled how they allocated responsibilities during food searches, food storage, food sharing, and defense. He studied animal "families," their relationships with their offspring, and how they held themselves together as a group. He published his findings in papers and articles.

Though he never really had adequate research facilities, Turner became a world-recognized authority on insect behavior. In the *Negro History Bulletin* (1939) it was stated: "What [Turner] learned about animals was made use of by other scientists in bringing out what they called behavioristic psychology. . . . Turner endeavored to see how their lives paralleled [those] of people."

At a memorial service held for Turner after his death in 1923, A. G. Pohlman of the Academy of Science of St. Louis said, "Permit me in the name of the Academy of Science to pay our respect not only to Turner the scientist but also to Turner the man." It is important to note that at the time, blacks were not admitted to the National Academy of Sciences due to their race. It wasn't until 1960 that the National Academy of Sciences admitted a black scientist, David H. Blackwell. Pohlman may have alluded to that fact when he went on to say, "No man is truly great unless he rises above the petty inconveniences of his surroundings: no man is strong unless he meets the competition around him. It is for you who knew Dr. Turner to satisfy yourself that here indeed was a great man."

Other Outstanding Life Scientists

There are many more African-American scientists who made notable contributions in the area of the life sciences since Turner's time. These are a few.

☐ In 1958, Robert Ewell Greene, Sr., a graduate of Lincoln and Howard universities, patented a "small animal retainer," or a "mouse tail holder." The device is used to restrain small lab animals for "intravenous injections into the lateral tail vein of the mouse." Though it seems a curious invention, veterinarians and biological researchers consider Greene's tool essential lab equipment.

☐ Leon Roddy (1922–   ), an entomologist, identified and cataloged six thousand spiders found around the world. Charles Parker (1882–19??), a botanist, discovered and described thirty-nine species of plants, and his research ended the blight of stoned fruit in Washington State in the 1920s.

And since the late 1960s Dr. Neal McAlpin's work as a professor and botanist at Tennessee State University has advanced our knowledge of orchids and other flowering plants.

☐ Dr. William Hinton (1883–1959) developed the famous Hinton test for the detection of syphilis. Dorothy McClendon, who began her career as a microbiologist in 1953, developed methods to keep oil and other materials free of bacteria and fungi.

In the tradition of these scientists, young African Americans are choosing careers in the life sciences in record numbers. Their contributions are adding to the proud heritage of those who were trailblazers.

4

OUT OF THE TUBE:
CHEMISTRY
AND PHYSICS

Since "chemistry" is the study of the utilization of natural substances and the creation of artificial ones, then cooking, fermentation, glass making, and metallurgy are all chemical processes that date back to the beginning of early human history. For centuries chemistry was considered the work of wizards and magicians. The alchemists of old spent their time searching for a formula that could change common metals into gold or an elixir of eternal life. Science had very little to do with their bubbling bottles and smoking vats.

Every now and then an alchemist would stumble upon a formula that was the basis of a real scientific breakthrough. Slowly alchemy evolved into chemistry, including pharmacology, the science dealing with the preparation, use, and effect of drugs. It wasn't until the late eighteenth century that modern chemistry was born. Today, chemical specializations include organic, inorganic, physical, analytical, industrial, and bio-chemistry.

Physics, the sister of chemistry, is a much older science and deals with matter, motion, and energy. Scientists have used the principles of physics in their teaching and research for centuries.

In 1965 there were 500,000 chemical substances, natural or artificial, that had been identified and pro-duced. By 1990 the number had increased to 8 million. Vinyl, Teflon, liquid crystals, and semiconductors are part of twentieth-century chemical technology, but computer chemists are paving the way for technical discoveries that boggle the mind.

Early African-American Chemists and Physicists

One of the first practicing African-American chemists was William G. Haynes. After the Civil War, he served as assistant chief chemist for the Union Pacific Rail-road, when a lot of African Americans were hired only as porters or spike drivers. He was responsible for the preparation of the liquid used to preserve railroad ties.

Lloyd Ferguson was the first African American to receive a Ph.D. in chemistry from the University of California at Berkley, in 1916, and St. Elmo Brady was the first to earn an advanced degree in physics at the University of Illinois, also in 1916. Ferguson wrote a chemistry textbook that was used in white and black colleges throughout the country.

It was in education that most black chemists and physicists left a mark of distinction. Dr. Julia M. Martin, an African-American woman, earned many honors for herself as a biochemist but also served as a role model for other women to emulate in the sciences. Dr. Robert P. Barnes inspired a generation of young scientists at Howard University. His former students, according to one source, were at one time "publishing more articles in the *Journal of the American Chemical Society* than all the chemistry professors in all of the black colleges combined." Halson Vashon Eagleson, James Raymond Lawson, and Cecil McBay, all professors of chemistry and physics, were award-winning educators whose students are today listed among the top industrial chemists in the country.

Other chemistry-related fields where blacks made impressive inroads were pharmacy and nutrition. Although a number of black people had owned and operated drugstores, the first African-American graduate pharmacist was Ray Clifford Darlington, who graduated from Ohio State in 1948. Cecile Edwards was a 1950 graduate in nutrition of Iowa State University who conducted research in amino acids. Flemmie Kittrell was the first black female to earn a Ph.D. in nutrition as a Fulbright scholar at Cornell University, in 1935. Her research was in early childhood health and nutrition.

The successes of these scientists can't be denied. But the National Inventors Hall of Fame has only inducted two African-American scientists, George Washington Carver and Percy L. Julian, a chemist, who has been called "the greatest of the great."

Greatest of the Great:
Dr. Percy Julian, Chemist

A Chicago newspaper called Percy Julian (1899–1975) "one of the best scientists in the country" without prefacing the statement with "black" or "African-American." Other than Benjamin Banneker, Percy Julian did more than anyone to shatter persistent stereotypes regarding racial inferiority at a time when discrimination was widespread. He earned wide acclaim for his work in the preparation of synthesized cortisone, a drug used to relieve millions who suffer from chronic arthritic pain.

Percy L. Julian was born in Montgomery, Alabama, on April 11, 1899. After completing grade school in Alabama, he had no money to seek higher education. Determined to get a degree, he made his way to DePauw University in Greencastle, Indiana, where he was accepted as a "provisional student" because he was too ill prepared to enter as a full freshman. He lived in the attic of a fraternity house and earned money doing chores.

Julian studied very hard and graduated in 1920, at the top of his class and as a Phi Beta Kappa honor student. Soon his parents moved to Chicago so that their other children might have benefit of the same educational opportunities.

Percy's two brothers and three sisters were also graduates of DePauw. Emerson Julian became a well-known physician, and Hubert Julian became one of only four blacks who were licensed to fly private aircraft in the early 1900s. (Hubert was known as the "Black

Percy Julian in his laboratory, where he developed dozens of uses for the soybean.

Eagle." During the Italian-Ethiopian War in 1935, he went to Ethiopia and offered his services to Emperor Haile Selassie.) Years later, the Julian children established a memorial fund at DePauw in honor of their parents and the sacrifices they made to educate them all.

After graduating from DePauw, Percy Julian taught at Fisk and Howard universities and West Virginia State College. He was granted an Austin Fellowship in chemistry in 1923, to work on his master's degree at Harvard University. He earned his doctorate in 1931 from the University of Vienna, where he studied under the well-known chemist Ernst Spaeth.

Returning to DePauw, he taught for a number of years, but he was denied promotions because of his race—in spite of the fact that in 1935 he had synthesized physostigmine, a drug used in the treatment of glaucoma and, more recently, Alzheimer's disease. He left to become director of research at Glidden Corporation in Chicago, a paint and varnish manufacturer, where he stayed for eighteen years, from 1936 to 1954.

Julian was to the soybean what George Washington Carver had been to the peanut. Julian found many ways to use the soybean, including the preparation of synthetic male and female hormones, weatherproof coverings for battleships, and a product that became the base of the foam fire extinguishers used in World War II. He was the holder of more than 138 chemical patents. Among the most important was his method of synthesizing cortisone, which made this drug available to the needy at a reasonable price.

Cortisone is used to treat arthritis and a variety of other serious conditions. Natural cortisone is taken from oxen bile and costs hundreds of dollars per ounce. Julian discovered that he could make cortisone inexpensively from sterols found in the babasco root, a wild yam that grows in Central America. Consequently, more people could be treated for severe arthritic pain.

Between 1953 and 1954, Julian left Glidden and founded Julian Laboratories, Inc., in Franklin Park, Illinois, and Mexico City, where he mass-produced drugs made from sterols found in soybeans. He sold the Franklin Park company to the Smith, Kline and French pharmaceutical company for several million dollars in 1961.

Julian was showered with many awards for his outstanding chemical achievements. Among them were the Spingarn Award, given to him by the NAACP in 1947, the "Chicagoan of the Year" award in 1950, and the Chemical Pioneer Award from the American Institute of Chemists. Dr. Percy Julian died on April 18, 1975, but his great works continue to make living better for millions of people everywhere.

Other Chemists and Physicists

Percy Julian was denied a professorship at a white university because of his race, but civil rights activists continued to chip away at segregation laws, which had been etched into a stone wall that kept black people from progressing. In time, unjust laws were struck down and replaced with new ones that were supposed to protect all Americans' rights. Encouraged by these changes, a new generation of well-educated black men and women stepped into positions that had previously been reserved for whites.

Julius H. Taylor earned a Ph.D. in solid-state physics from the University of Pennsylvania in 1950. He taught at several mostly white universities and conducted research with grants from the Office of Ordnance Research, U.S. Army, from 1953 to 1957. He wrote several articles that were published in professional journals. And John William Lathen, who was the first black hired at Bendix Corporation as a metallurgical chemist, paved the way for other industrial chemists who followed him.

J. Ernest Wilkins, Jr., was the son of J. Ernest Wilkins, Sr., who was appointed by Dwight D. Eisenhower as assistant secretary of labor and was the first African American to be appointed to a subcabinet position. Wilkins, Jr., was born in 1923 in Chicago, Illinois. After earning his Ph.D. in mathematics in 1942, he served as a physicist on the Manhattan Project at the University of Chicago from 1944 to 1946, helping to develop the atomic bomb.

When World War II ended, he worked for the American Optical Company and the Nuclear Development Corporation of America. Then he moved to General Dynamics, where he was the director of the Department of Theoretical Physics from 1960 to 1965. He also taught mathematics and physics at Howard University.

Lincoln I. Diuguid (pronounced Do-Good) was not treated as well by the scientific world when he began his career as a chemist in 1947. Diuguid graduated with honors from Cornell University with a Ph.D. in organic chemistry and finished two years of post-doctorate work. But even these impressive credentials couldn't land him a good job.

"In 1947, there were very few jobs for blacks or Jews," said Diuguid. And if companies did hire blacks, according to Diuguid, "they put you in a corner and told you to be quiet."

After his post-doctorate work Diuguid was approached by a chewing-gum company executive, who offered him a position as assistant research director, but he had to agree not to let anybody know he was black or to hire another African American. Diuguid, who is a fair-skinned black, could have easily hidden his racial identity, but he chose not to accept the offer.

Instead Diuguid joined the staff of Harris-Stowe State College in St. Louis, Missouri, where he taught science for thirty-three years. After retiring in 1982, Diuguid devoted all his time to DU-GOOD Laboratories, his own chemical research company. In his small, second-story lab, cluttered with test tubes, he developed detergents, a hand cleanser, dry-cleaning fluid, aftershave lotion, and mosquito repellent.

Diuguid likens his life to that of Plato, a famous Greek philosopher. "The King of Sparta," he said leaning back in his large armchair, "once told Plato that he should be a king living in a castle. And Plato replied, 'I'd rather be a king in a cabin than a slave in a castle.' "

Although many of his classmates at Cornell became presidents of companies or were involved in important government projects, Diuguid believes his work as a teacher was important, too. During his years as a professor he helped prepare students for the challenges that faced them in an ever-changing world.

Shirley Ann Jackson, a gifted black nuclear physicist, represents the spirit and hope of a new generation of African-American scientists that Diuguid and others like him helped to train. They are prepared to take their rightful place on the team of scientists who will take the world into the twenty-first century.

You Can Do It, Too!
Dr. Shirley Ann
Jackson, Physicist

Shirley Ann Jackson (1946–) is an outstanding scientist who is making important contributions in theoretical physics. In a biographical sketch in *Epic Lives*, contributing author Jesse Carney Smith called Jackson "one of today's most distinguished young black American scientists."

Born in Washington, D.C., at the dawning of the nuclear age, Jackson was encouraged by her family to be whatever she wanted to be. She graduated valedictorian in 1964 from Roosevelt High School, and in 1973 was the first woman to earn a Ph.D. in physics from Massachusetts Institute of Technology. She studied under Dr. James Young, who was the first full-time tenured black professor in the MIT physics department. Her area of expertise has taken her to the European Center for Nuclear Research in Geneva, Switzerland, the International School of Subnuclear Physics in Erice, Sicily, and the Ecole D'Éte de Physique Theorique in Les Houches, France, where she worked on theories of strongly interacting elementary particles—that is, nuclear physics.

*Physicist Shirley Ann Jackson's message
to students is "believe in yourself."*

Jackson worked at AT&T Bell Laboratories in Murray Hill, New Jersey, where she conducted research on theoretical material sciences, and for her work she has won many awards and fellowships.

Asked what advice she would give young students who were considering careers in science, she told a reporter, "I would say believe in yourself. Plant it in your head, 'I can do it.' And you can do it, too!"

BIBLIOGRAPHY

BOOKS

Adams, Russell L. *Great Negroes Past and Present*. Chicago: Afro-Am Publishing Company, 1984.

Aptheker, Herbert. *A Documentary History of the Negro People in the United States*, vols. 1, 2, 3, and 4. New York: Citadel Press, 1973, Carol Publishing Group, 1990.

Asante, Molefi, and Mark T. Mattson. *Historical and Cultural Atlas of African Americans*. New York: Macmillan, 1992.

Asimov, Isaac. *The Wall Chart of Science and Invention: The Growth of Human Knowledge from Pre-History to Space Travel*. New York: Dorset Press, 1991.

Bennett, Lerone, Jr. *Before the Mayflower: A History of Black America*, 6th ed. Chicago: Johnson Publishing, 1988.

Haber, Louis. *Black Pioneers of Science and Invention*. New York: Harcourt Brace Jovanovich, 1970.

Hayden, Robert. *Seven Black American Scientists*. New York: Addison-Wesley, 1970.

Hornsby, Alton, Jr. *Chronology of African American History*. Detroit: Gale Research, 1991.

Jay, James M. *Negroes in Science: Natural Science Doctorates, 1876–1969*. Detroit: Balamp Publishers, 1971.

Low, W. Augustus, and Virgil A. Clift, ed. *Encyclopedia of Black America*. New York: McGraw Hill, 1981, A DA CAPO (paperback edition), 1984.

The Macmillan Visual Dictionary, 1992.

Page One: Major Events as Presented in the New York Times Newspaper—1920–1982. New York: Arno Press, 1982.

Sammons, Vivian Ovelton. *Blacks in Science and Medicine*. New York: Hemisphere Publishing, 1990.

Smith, Jessie Carney. *Epic Lives: One Hundred Black Women Who Made a Difference*. Detroit: Visible Ink Press, 1993.

Williams, James C. *At Last Recognition in America*, vol. 1, *A Reference Handbook of Unknown Black Inventors and Their Contributions to America*. Chicago: B.C.C. Publishing, 1978.

ARTICLES

Baker Henry. "Benjamin Banneker, The Negro Mathematician and Astronomer." *Journal of Negro History*, vol. 3, no. 2 (April 1918).

"The Negro in the Beginning of Science, May 1939," *The Afro-American History Kit*. Washington, D.C.: Associated Publishers, 1992.

"Sketches of a Few Greats and Near Greats." *The Afro-American History Kit*. Washington, D.C.: Associated Publishers, 1992.

INDEX

ABOUT THE AUTHORS

Patricia and Fredrick McKissack are well-known authors of children's books. Among their many acclaimed nonfiction works are numerous biographies, including *Sojourner Truth: Ain't I a Woman,* and *The Civil Rights Movement in America From 1865 to the Present,* a history that is used in junior high and middle schools all over the country. In 1990, the McKissacks combined their talents to write *A Long Hard Journey: The Story of the Pullman Porter,* which won both the Coretta Scott King Award and the Jane Addams Peace Award. They have also written beginning-reader and picture books, and have served as editors for several series. Among Patricia's well-received books are *Jesse Jackson: A Biography* and *The Dark-Thirty: Southern Tales of the Supernatural.* Both McKissacks are 1964 Tennessee State graduates, and Pat earned a master's degree in early childhood education at Webster University in St. Louis, Missouri. The McKissacks live in St. Louis.